D1547602

NEW BELIEVER'S SERIES

WATCHMAN NEE

LEADING MEN TO CHRIST

Living Stream Ministry
Anaheim, California

5

First Edition, November 1997.

ISBN 1-57593-961-4

Published by

Living Stream Ministry
2431 W. La Palma Ave., Anaheim, CA 92801 U.S.A.
P. O. Box 2121, Anaheim, CA 92814 U.S.A.

Printed in the United States of America

00   01   02   03   04   05   /   10   9   8   7   6   5   4   3   2

LEADING MEN TO CHRIST

Scripture Reading: Rom. 1:16; 10:14; 1 Tim. 2:1, 4; Mark 16:15

In the previous chapter we said that once a person believes in the Lord, he has to witness for the Lord. In this chapter we want to talk about the ways to lead men to Christ. If we do not know how to lead people to Christ, I am afraid that much of our witnessing will be in vain. There are several things which we must do and learn if we want to lead men to Christ. We can group them into two categories: First, going to God on man's behalf, and second, going to man on God's behalf. In addition, we would also like to say something about passing out tracts.

I. GOING TO GOD ON MAN'S BEHALF

A. Prayer Being the Foundation of Leading Men to Christ

There is a foundational work in leading men to Christ. Before one opens his mouth before man, he first must open his mouth before God. We need to first ask God and then talk to men. We always need to talk to God first, not man. Some brothers and sisters are very zealous to lead men to Christ, but they do not pray for them. A man may have great interest in people, but if he has no burden to pray before the Lord, his work of saving souls will be ineffectual. A person must have a burden before the Lord before he can witness to men.

The Lord Jesus said, "All that the Father gives Me will come to Me, and him who comes to Me I shall by no means cast out" (John 6:37). According to Acts 2:47, the Lord added to the church daily those who were being saved. The first thing that we must do is ask God for people, asking Him to give men to the Lord Jesus and to add them to the church. In order for men to be saved, we need to ask God and implore Him. It is very difficult to deal with man's heart. It is not easy for us to turn a heart toward the Lord. We must first go to God and pray for these people, asking God to bind the strong man (Luke 11:21-22). Afterwards, we can talk to them at length. We have to present these people one by one to the Lord and pray for them fervently before we can effectively lead them to Christ.

Those who are good at leading men to Christ are good at prayer. If you have trouble getting answers to prayer, you will have trouble witnessing for the Lord. If you have no confidence in prayer, you will have no confidence in leading men to Christ. Hence, you must learn to pray in a practical way and not let this matter slip by.

B. Preparing a Record Book

In order to pray for people in a proper way, you should keep a record book. Allow God to put the names of those whom He wishes to save in your heart. When you were first saved, how did you know to whom you should go to make restitution? How did you know whom you should repay? It was the Lord who put the person's name in your heart and who reminded you of particular things. This reminder compelled you to make restitution with others. One day you suddenly thought of something. Another day something else came to your mind. As a result of this enlightening, you dealt with these things one by one. The same principle holds true in leading men to Christ. Allow the Lord to put some names in your heart. When these names are in your heart, spontaneously you will be burdened to pray for them. The Lord may put a few people or a few dozen people in your heart. In writing these names down, the most important thing to remember is to take the names that the Lord has put in your heart. Do not sit down and simply make out a list at random. You will be wasting your time if you mindlessly write down something. Your success will be dependent upon how good your start is. You have to ask God specifically for a few names. Out of all your family members, friends, colleagues, schoolmates, and those whom you know, a few names will spontaneously come to your mind. You will have a feeling for them, and you will want them to be saved first.

A record book should have the following columns: The first column should be a number; the second column, the date; and the third column, the name. This will remind us of the number we have assigned to a person and the date we began to pray for him. The fourth column should also be a date—the date when the person is saved. If the person unfortunately dies, we can put the date of death in this column. One should persist and not give up once a name is in the book. The prayer for a person should follow him until he dies. If the person is alive and not saved, you should keep on praying for him until he is saved. One brother prayed for his friend for eighteen years before his friend was saved. It is not certain when a person will be saved. Some are saved in a year, and some in two to three months. Perhaps one or two of them may prove to be very difficult, but in the end they will still be saved. You should not relax but relentlessly pursue in prayer for their salvation.

C. The Greatest Obstacle to Prayer Being Sin

Prayer is a test; it exposes your spiritual condition before the Lord. If your spiritual condition is proper and normal, others will be saved one by one. As you intercede continuously before the Lord, you may find one or two persons saved after a few days or half a month. After a while, another three or five may be saved. People should be saved regularly. If your prayers are not answered for a long time, it must mean that you are sick before the Lord. You should go to the Lord for light and find out where your problem lies.

The greatest obstacle to prayer is sin. We must learn to live a holy life before the Lord. We must reject all known sins. The moment we take sin lightly or tolerate it, our prayers will be hindered.

Sin has both an objective aspect and a subjective aspect. The objective aspect has to do with God, while the subjective aspect has to do with us. On the objective side, sin obstructs God's grace and promises. Isaiah 59:1-2 says, "Behold,

Jehovah's hand is not so short that it cannot save; / Nor is His ear so heavy that it cannot hear. / But your iniquities have become a separation / Between you and your God, / And your sins have hidden His face / From you so that He does not hear." Psalm 66:18 says, "If I regard iniquity in my heart, / The Lord will not hear." If a person does not take care of the problem of sin properly, he will find hindrance to his prayer. Unconfessed sins, sins which are never dealt with by the blood, are a big obstacle before God; they are the cause of unanswered prayer. This is on the objective side.

On the subjective side, sin damages man's conscience. When a person sins, no matter what he says to himself, how much he reads the Bible, how many promises there are in the Word, how much grace God has, and how much He accepts him, his conscience will be weakened and bound. First Timothy 1:19 says, "Holding faith and a good conscience, concerning which some, thrusting these away, have become shipwrecked regarding the faith." A ship may be old or small, but it cannot leak. Similarly, our conscience must not have a leak. As soon as the conscience is not at peace, many prayers cannot be uttered. Thus, there are obstacles not only before God but even within man himself. The relationship between faith and conscience is just like that between a ship and its cargo. Faith is like the cargo, and the conscience is like a ship. When the ship has a leak, the cargo will be damaged. When the conscience is strong, faith will be strong. But when there is a leak in the conscience, faith will be gone. If our heart blames us, God is greater than our heart and knows all things (1 John 3:20).

If you want to be a man of prayer, you must deal with sin thoroughly. You lived in sin for a long time in the past. If you are not careful with it now, you will not be totally free from it. You have to deal with sin seriously; you have to come before God to confess every sin, putting every sin under the blood, refusing it, and coming out from it. Then your conscience will be recovered. As soon as the blood cleanses, the conscience is recovered. There will be no condemnation, and spontaneously you will see God's face. Never give in to sin. This will weaken you before the Lord. If you are weak before the Lord, you will not be able to intercede for others. As long as sin remains, you will not be able to utter anything in your prayer. Sin is the number one problem. You should pay attention to it all the time, even daily. If one deals with sin properly before the Lord, he will be able to offer proper prayers, and others will be brought to the Lord through him.

D. Praying with Faith

Another important thing is to have faith in our prayers. If the conscience is blameless, it is easy for faith to be strong, and if faith is strong, spontaneously our prayers will be answered.

What is faith? Faith is freedom from doubt. It is to accept God's promises in our prayers. It is God who asks us to pray and who wants us to pray. God said, "Concerning the work of My hands, command Me" (Isa. 45:11). If we pray, God has to answer us. Jesus said, "Knock and it shall be opened to you" (Matt. 7:7). It is impossible for Him not to open after we have knocked. Jesus said, "Seek and you shall find." It is impossible for us not to find after we have sought. Jesus said, "Ask and it shall be given to you." It is impossible for us to ask and yet not receive. If we do not believe this, what kind of God do we think our God is? We must see that God's promises are faithful and dependable. Faith is based on our knowledge of God. The more we know God, the stronger our faith will be. We are saved already; we know God already. Therefore, we can believe; there should not be any difficulty at all for us to believe. When we believe, God will answer our prayers. Learn to be a person full of faith from the very beginning. We should not trust in our feelings or our mind. Instead, we should believe in God's word. God's promises are like cash; they work. In fact, God's promises are God's work. The promises tell us of God's work, while His work is the manifestation of His promises. We have to accept God's promises in the same way we accept His work. When we believe God's word, abiding in faith rather than in doubt, we will see how real God's words are and we will find answers to our prayers.

E. Aspiring to Be a Praying Person

We need to have the ambition to be a praying person, a

person with power before God. Some people are powerful before God, while others are not. When some people speak, God listens. When others speak, He does not listen. What does it mean to be powerful before God? It simply means that God listens to the person when he speaks. It is as if God is happy to be influenced by such a one. Some people can influence God. Being powerless before God means that God does not listen to the person when he speaks. Such a one may spend much time before God, but God ignores him. We must have the desire and the aspiration to see that God often answers our prayers. No blessing can be greater than God answering our prayers all the time. We have to pray to Him, "May every request of ours be pleasing to Your ears." It is a most glorious thing for God to incline His ear to us. It is a tremendous thing for God to trust us to the extent that He can give us whatever we ask.

You have to present to the Lord the names that you are burdened with and pray for them one by one. See how long it takes for God to save them. If your prayers are unanswered after a long period, you have to deal with yourself and with God. In order for your prayers to be answered, it is often necessary to go through specific dealings. Unanswered prayer means that there is sickness somewhere. If you do not mean business in this matter, you will always fail.

This is why you need a record book. The record book will show you whether or not your prayers are answered. Many people do not know whether their prayers are answered because they do not have a record of anything. Newly saved brothers and sisters should learn to have such a record book. Then they will know whether or not their prayers are answered. They will know whether there is a problem between them and the Lord. They will know also when they have to deal with themselves and when they have to deal with God.

If you have prayed for a long time and there is still no answer, you should realize that there must be some hindrance. The hindrances always occur because there is sin in your conscience or there is a problem with your faith. New believers need not worry about the deeper aspects of prayer. They need only to pay attention to their conscience and their faith. Before the Lord, we have to confess, deal with, and refuse our sins. At the same time we have to genuinely and fully trust in God's promises. If we do this, we will see people being saved one by one, and our lives will be full of answers to prayer.

F. Praying Daily

You have to pray for those around you. Is there no one who needs your prayers? How many colleagues do you have? How many neighbors do you have? How many relatives and friends do you have? Always ask the Lord to place one or two special persons in your heart. When the Lord places a person in your heart, He intends to save this person through you. You should write down his name in your record book and continually bring him to the Lord through prayer.

You need to set aside a fixed time daily for this work of intercession. Whether it be an hour, half an hour, or a quarter of an hour, it must be a fixed time. If there is no fixed time for prayer, there will not be definite prayer. As a result, there will not be any prayer at all. Hence, always fix a time for prayers, whether it is a quarter of an hour or half an hour. Do not be too ambitious; do not plan for two hours and end up not being able to carry it out. It is more practical to set aside one hour, half an hour, or a quarter of an hour. Always fix a time to pray for those who need your prayer. Do not relax. Do this every day. After a while, you will see sinners saved one by one.

G. A Few Examples of Intercession

We will mention a few stories here to show you how others have done this work.

1. A Boiler Worker

Once a boiler worker in a ship was saved. He asked the brother who led him to Christ, "Please tell me the first thing that I must do for the Lord?" The brother replied, "The Lord will choose a few of your companions and put them in your heart. You will have to pray for them." There were more than ten persons working together at his place. He remembered one person in particular and prayed for him daily. That person found out about this, and he became angry. Later, an evangelist came by and preached the gospel to the men there. After the meeting he stood up and said, "I want to believe in Jesus." The evangelist asked, "Why do you want to believe in Jesus?" He said, "A person has been praying for me for some time. I have to believe in Jesus." The boiler worker had been praying for this man. Although he did not like this in the beginning, the power of prayer overcame him, and in the end he accepted the Lord.

2. A Sixteen-year-old Youth

A sixteen-year-old youth was working as a copy writer in a construction firm. The chief engineer of the company had a very bad temper and almost everyone was afraid of him. After the youth was saved, he started to pray for the chief engineer. He was afraid of the engineer and dared not open his mouth, yet he prayed earnestly for him daily. After a short while, the engineer asked him, "I have over two hundred people in the company, but I feel that you are different. Can you please tell me why you and I are so different?" The engineer was about forty to fifty years old, and the youth was only sixteen. The young man answered, "I have believed in the Lord, and you have not." The engineer immediately said, "I also want to believe in Him." The youth brought him to the church, and the engineer was saved.

3. Two Sisters

In Europe there are guest houses which are open to strangers. They are not hotels, but they receive travelers. Once there were two Christian sisters whose house was open to travelers. Sometimes, as many as twenty or thirty would stay at their place. They noticed the luxury of the travelers' attire and the vanity of their conversation. The sisters were bothered and wanted to win them over to Christ. However, there were many guests and only two of them. How could they win them over? They decided to sit at the two ends of the room during the conversation and pray for the guests from each end.

On the first day during the after-dinner conversation, each

sister sat at one end, praying for the guests one by one. One prayed from one end, and the other prayed from the other end. They prayed for each and every one of them. This stopped the guests' jesting and chatting on that first day. They asked themselves what had happened. On that day, one person was saved. The next day, another lady was saved. One by one they were gradually all brought to the Lord.

Prayer is indispensable. The first condition in bringing people to the Lord is intercessory prayer. We must pray systematically, orderly, daily, and relentlessly, until our friends are saved.

II. GOING TO MAN ON GOD'S BEHALF

Merely going to God on man's behalf is not enough. We also have to go to man on God's behalf. We have to tell men about God. Many people have the courage to speak to God, but they have no courage to speak to man. We have to exercise boldness to speak to men. We have to tell them the kind of Lord our Lord is. When we speak, we need to pay attention to a few things.

A. Never Engaging in Useless Arguments

First, never engage in useless arguments. This does not mean that there should never be any arguments. Acts tells us of a few arguments. Even Paul argued (cf. Acts 17:2, 17-18; 18:4, 19). However, useless arguments do not save people. Sometimes it is all right to engage in arguments. But this is mainly for the benefit of other listeners. Try to avoid arguing with the ones you are trying to save because arguments often drive people away instead of bringing them in. If you argue with them, they will run away.

Many people think that arguments can touch men's hearts. Actually, this never happens. At the most, arguments can convince men's minds. Their mouths may be shut, but their hearts will not be won over. Arguments produce little result. Try to say less in the way of argument and more in the way of testimony. You have only to tell others that you felt happy and peaceful after you believed in the Lord Jesus, that you sleep well now, and that even meals are becoming tastier. No one can argue with you about these things. They can only wonder. You have to show them that they do not have your kind of peace and joy and that they should therefore believe in the Lord.

B. Keeping to the Facts

The key to leading men to the Lord is to emphasize the facts, not the doctrines. Just recall what it was like when you were saved. You did not believe because you understood the doctrines. Many people understand the doctrines, but they do not believe. It is impossible for any brother to try to lead others to Christ through arguments and doctrines. The key to leading men to Christ is to keep to the facts. This is why simple ones often are more effective in leading others to the Lord; those who are good at doctrines may not lead others to the Lord. Some people can give wonderful messages. But what use is there in winning the minds of others, if one cannot help them be saved?

Once there was an old man who considered going to church a good habit. He was not saved, yet he would go to church every Sunday and also make his whole family go. But when he returned home, he would lose his temper, and all kinds of bad words would come out of his mouth. The whole family was afraid of him. One day his daughter, who was a believer, came to visit him. She brought her little daughter with her. The old man brought the little granddaughter to the church. When they came out of the church, the little granddaughter looked at her grandfather and felt that he did not look like a believer. She asked him, "Do you believe in Jesus?" The grandfather said, "Children should keep their mouths shut." After walking a few steps, she said to her grandfather again, "You do not look as if you have believed in Jesus." Again the old man said, "Children should keep their mouths shut." After a while she asked her grandfather, "Why do you not believe in Jesus?" This little child saw a fact—the way her grandfather attended church was different from the way other believers attended church. The old man, who was otherwise wild and hard to deal with, became soft after his little granddaughter's probing questions. On that day he accepted the Lord.

The preaching of the gospel requires skill. One must know the way God works before he can preach the gospel. A person may preach the right doctrines, and crowds of people may come for his messages, but the same crowds may walk away unsaved. You will not get any fish with a straight hook. The fishing hook must be curved before one can catch fish. Those who lead others to the Lord need to know how to use a hook. Use only the words that can catch people. If your words cannot catch people, try to change the way you speak. Facts are words that catch; they are words that can touch others.

C. Being Sincere in Attitude

Do not delve into many teachings. Try to speak more facts. At the same time, be sincere in attitude. Saving a man's soul is not a light matter. I once saw a person who wanted to lead others to the Lord. He was willing to pray, but his attitude was wrong. He joked around as he spoke about the Lord. Whatever spiritual power he might have had was lost through his jokes. As a result, he could not lead anyone to the Lord. One has to be very sincere in his attitude. He must not be flippant or funny in his attitude. He has to let others see that this is the most serious matter in the whole world.

D. Praying for the Opportunity to Speak

You also need to pray unceasingly for God to provide you with the right opportunity to speak. When you pray, God will give you the opportunity.

One sister gathered a group of women together once a week and led them in a Bible study. The women all worked in the same company, and none of them believed in the Lord. One of them was very particular about her dress. She was very proud and would not listen to anything the sister said. The sister took notice of her and prayed for her. She asked God to give her the opportunity to speak to the woman. One day she felt a desire to invite the woman over for tea. Since this woman loved to socialize, she accepted the invitation. When she came, the sister encouraged her to believe in the Lord. She replied, "I cannot believe. I like to gamble, and I love pleasure. I do not want to lose these things. I cannot believe in Jesus." The sister said, "If a person wants to believe in the Lord Jesus, she has to stop gambling. Anyone who wants to believe in the Lord Jesus must give up vainglory. You have to give up these things if you want to believe in the Lord Jesus." The woman said, "The price is too high. I cannot afford it." The sister said, "I hope you will go back and consider it." After she said this, she continued to pray for her. The woman returned home and knelt down to pray. After she prayed, she suddenly said, "I have decided to follow the Lord Jesus today." She changed suddenly. She could not explain it, but her heart just turned. She changed her attire; she no longer dressed the same as before. Wonderful things followed one after another. Within a year many of her colleagues were brought to the Lord one by one.

You may think that it is difficult to talk to someone, but if you pray for him, the Lord will give you the opportunity to speak to him, and he will change. The sister who was having Bible studies had been afraid to speak to the woman because the woman behaved as though she knew everything and could do everything. She appeared to be very arrogant, but the Lord gave this sister the burden to pray for her. One day the Lord told the sister to speak to her. She put aside her considerations and spoke to her. You have to pray on the one hand and learn to open your mouth on the other. After you have prayed for a person for some time, the Lord will impress you to speak to him. You will have to tell him about the Lord's grace and the things that He has done for you. He will not be able to resist you because he cannot oppose the things that the Lord has done for you. The newly saved brothers and sisters must pray daily for the Lord to provide opportunities to speak to others. What a pity that some people have been saved for several years already, yet they dare not open their mouths to speak to their relatives and friends! Perhaps your fear has caused you to miss many opportunities that were waiting for you.

E. Speaking in Season and out of Season

We mentioned earlier that you must pray before you speak

to a person. This, however, does not mean that you cannot speak if you have not prayed. You have to speak to men even if you are seeing them for the first time. Always grasp the opportunity to speak, whether in season or out of season. You never know who you are missing. Speak whenever there is the chance. Always be prepared to open your mouth. Of course, first and foremost, you have to pray for those whose names appear in your record book. But you have to pray for those whom you do not know. You should pray, "Lord, please save the sinners. Whoever they may be, please save them." Whenever you meet someone and have an urge in your heart to speak, you should speak to him.

If we do not heed this urging, we may let a soul slip away from us. We should not let so many souls slip through our hands. We hope that all the brothers and sisters will testify faithfully for the Lord and bring many to Christ.

F. Studying Carefully

Each time you lead someone to the Lord, you have to do a detailed analysis, just like a doctor who studies each patient's case in detail. The doctor cannot prescribe the same medicine to everyone. Certain sicknesses require certain drugs. He administers a particular drug to a particular patient. The same is true in leading men to Christ. No one can be a doctor without studying medicine. In the same way, no one can lead men to the Lord without studying. Some brothers and sisters are good at bringing people to the Lord because they have studied the ones whom they brought to the Lord. At the beginning of the work of leading men to Christ, a new believer has to work hard to study each case. You should always study why a particular person accepted the Lord. Why did a particular word open him up? Why did another person not believe after hearing a particular word? Why did a person shy away after listening attentively for a while? Why did a person accept when he earlier had opposed? Why are there no fish after waiting for a long time? We always have to find the reason that the Spirit is working, and we also have to find the reason that the Spirit is not working.

If you fail to lead men to Christ, do not put all the blame

on others. Those who are good at leading people to the Lord always look for problems within themselves. We cannot wait by the seaside and hope that the fish will jump to the shore. Leading people to the Lord is not so simple. We have to spend time to study and learn where the problems lie. Leading people to the Lord is a skill, and this skill is acquired through working with people. There is always something we can learn, whether through failure or success. Through failure, we learn the reason for our failure. Through success, we learn the reason for our success. In every situation, we need to study the reasons behind the results.

If you do this conscientiously, you will learn many lessons. Eventually, you will discover an interesting thing—as far as believing in the Lord is concerned, there are only a few types of people in the world. If you meet a certain type of person, you will need only to speak certain words to him, and he will receive the Lord. If you speak something else to him, he will oppose you and not believe. If you know how to handle these few types of people, you can handle most people. You can handle those whose names are in your record book, and you can handle those whom you come across by accident. As soon as you come across someone, you will take the opportunity to witness to him, and you will be able to tell immediately the type of person he is. You will know in your heart what to do with this type of person and how to speak to him. He will most likely be saved. If you study your cases one by one, you will become a very skillful soul-winner after one or two years. You will realize that soul winning takes wisdom. By God's mercy, you may lead some to the Lord, maybe a few dozen, or even a few hundred. If you study all these cases carefully, you will become a very powerful soul-winner.

APPENDIX:
PASSING OUT TRACTS

A. No Time Limit

During the past two to three hundred years, the Lord has used tracts in a particular way to save many people. One thing special about winning people with tracts is that tracts are not limited by time. If you try to testify with your mouth, you are restricted by time and personnel. You cannot speak twenty-four hours a day, and your audience may not be available all the time. You may be preaching a wonderful message, but the audience may not be there. However, tracts are not limited by time. You can pass out tracts any time of the day, and men can receive and read your tracts any time of the day. Today many people do not have the time to come to our meeting. But tracts are not limited by time. We can give them out to people who are walking on the streets, who are cooking in their kitchens, or who are working in their offices. This is the first convenience that tracts afford.

B. Tracts Can Convey the Gospel in Full

Many people are very zealous in testifying for the Lord and leading men to Christ. However, their knowledge is limited and their words are lacking. They cannot convey the gospel message adequately and fully. In addition to leading men to Christ through other means, a new believer has to do his best to select some good tracts in his spare time and pass them out to others. This will enable him to do what he himself could not do otherwise.

C. Tracts Not Being Affected by Human Factors

There is another advantage to using tracts. In preaching the gospel, sometimes we feel too shy to use strong words in front of people. Tracts do not have this inconvenience. They can go to anyone and say anything they want. A living preacher is often restricted by circumstances. But the preaching of the tracts is not affected by any human factors. New believers should learn to sow seeds with the tracts.

D. Passing Out Tracts Being a Way of Sowing

Another advantage of passing out tracts is that one can sow anywhere. The Old Testament says that we should sow our seed in many waters (Num. 24:7). It takes a considerable effort to speak to three, five, or ten persons together. But there is no difficulty in passing out a thousand, two thousand, or three thousand tracts a day. If one person can be saved out of the thousand tracts we pass out, this is wonderful enough. New believers should learn to pass out tracts in large quantities.

E. God Saving Men through Tracts

God has indeed used tracts to save people. I know of some people who slip tracts under doors. Others drop them into mailboxes. I remember an incident in which a person received a tract and then threw it away on the street. Another person, who had a nail stuck in his shoe, was looking for something to cushion his foot. He picked up the tract and stuffed it in his shoe. He returned home and began to mend his shoe. Then he saw the tract and was saved. There are numerous similar cases of people being saved by tracts. Some of these cases are actually quite marvelous.

F. Much Prayer and Dedication of Heart

A newly saved brother always should have tracts ready in his pockets, and he should pass them out when he is free. Like the work of leading men to Christ, we should do this with much prayer and dedication of heart. While we are passing out tracts, we can speak a word or two to others or we can remain silent. Either way is good. If a new believer practices this, he will receive great benefit from it.